Celery Juice Recipes That Don't Taste Gross

47 Healthy and Balanced Celery Juice Recipes for Beauty, Weight Loss and Energy

By Elena Garcia

Copyright Elena Garcia © 2019

Sign up for new books, fresh tips, super healthy recipes, and our latest wellness releases:

www.YourWellnessBooks.com

All rights reserved. No part of this publication may be reproduced, stored in a retrieval system, or transmitted, in any form or by any means, electronic, mechanical, photocopying, recording or otherwise, without the prior written permission of the author and the publishers.

The scanning, uploading, and distribution of this book via the Internet or via any other means without the permission of the author are illegal and punishable by law. Please purchase only authorized electronic editions, and do not participate in or encourage electronic piracy of copyrighted materials.

Disclaimer

A physician has not written the information in this book. It is advisable that you visit a qualified dietician so that you can obtain a highly personalized treatment for your case, especially if you want to lose weight effectively. This book is for informational and educational purposes only and is not intended for medical purposes. Please consult your physician before making any drastic changes to your diet.

All information in this book has been carefully researched and checked for factual accuracy. However, the author and publishers make no warranty, expressed or implied, that the information contained herein is appropriate for every individual, situation or purpose, and assume no responsibility for errors or omission. The reader assumes the risk, and full responsibility for all actions and the author will not be held liable for any loss or damage, whether consequential, incidental, and special or otherwise, that may result from the information presented in this publication.

The book is not intended to provide medical advice or to take the place of medical advice and treatment from your personal physician. Readers are advised to consult their own doctors or other qualified health professionals regarding the treatment of medical conditions. The author shall not be held liable or responsible for any misunderstanding or misuse of the information contained in this book. The information is not intended to diagnose, treat, or cure any disease.

If you suffer from any medical condition, are pregnant, lactating, or on medication, be sure to talk to your doctor before making any drastic changes in your diet and lifestyle.

Contents

Introduction – No More Celery Juice Hype 9

Juicing Recipes- Food Lists 14

    Recommended Fruit 14

    Other Fruit (in moderation) 14

    Recommended Greens to Use in Your Juicing Recipes 15

    Vegetables to Use in Your Juices: 16

    Spices & Herbs for Your Juices 17

    Natural Sweeteners and Supplements (Optional) 18

    Good Fats 19

    Other: 20

Your Wellness Books Email Newsletter 21

About the Recipes-Measurements Used in the Recipes 22

Celery Juice Recipes to Help You Thrive! 23

    Recipe#1 Avocado Oil Celery Juice for Energy & Weight Loss 25

    Recipe#2 Quit Sugar Cravings Juice 26

    Recipe#3 Celery Juice Glow 27

    Recipe#4 Celery Immune Tonic 28

    Recipe#5 Super Hydrating Weight Loss Juice 29

    Recipe#6 Holistic Balance Celery Juice 30

    Recipe#7 On the Go Celery Juice Shot (Liver Lover) 31

    Recipe#8 Easy Energy Reboot Juice 32

    Recipe#9 Aroma Detox Mix 33

    Recipe#10 Vitamin C Celery Juice for Natural Energy & Weight Loss .34

    Recipe#11 Light Alkaline Keto Juice 35

    Recipe#12 Apple Cider Antioxidant Juice for Optimal Energy 36

    Recipe#13 Herbal Weight Loss Juice 38

Recipe#14 Sleep Well Celery Juice 39

Recipe#15 Pomegranate Celery Anti-Sugar Cravings Juice 40

Recipe#16 Alkalizing Mojito Juice 41

Recipe #17 Cucumber Kale and Carrot Juice 42

Recipe #18 Flavored Celery Juice 43

Recipe #19 Watermelon Antioxidant Juice 44

Recipe #20 Simple Apple Lemon Juice 45

Recipe #21 Honeydew Melon Green Juice 46

Recipe #22 Easy Celery Juice 47

Recipe #23 Coconut Celery Concoction 48

Recipe #24 Broccoli and Orange Juice 49

Recipe #25 Green Tea High Energy Juice 50

Recipe #26 A Beta Carotene Powerhouse 51

Recipe #27 A Restorative Antioxidant Juice 52

Recipe #28 Veggie Medley Juice 53

Recipe #29 Coconut Flavored Antioxidant Juice 54

Recipe #30 Mixed Green Juice 55

Recipe #31 Tantalizing Green Juice 56

Recipe #32 Healing Carrot Juice 57

Recipe #33 Cucumber's Delight 58

Recipe #34 Turmeric Celery Juice 59

Recipe #35 Pineapple Lime Mint Juice 60

Recipe #36 Antioxidant Nutrition Juice 61

Recipe #37 Coconut Flavored Green Juice 62

Recipe#38 Creamy, Anti-Inflammatory Breakfast Delight 63

Recipe#39 Get Energized Antioxidant Juice 65

Recipe#40 Green Balance Party Juice 66

Recipe#41 Delicious Creamy Beet Juice 67

Recipe #42 Spicy Green Celery Juice 68

Recipe #43 Gazpacho Celery Juice 69

Recipe #44 "Replenish Yourself" Juice 70

Recipe #45 "Red Pepper Detox" Juice 71

Recipe #46 "Liver Lover" Juice 72

Recipe #47 Creamy Chia Juice 73

More Wellness Books & Resources 77

Content Disclaimer 78

Introduction – No More Celery Juice Hype

Yes, celery juice can be good for us, we have all heard it before.

But it can also be very harmful when overdone. And pure celery juice doesn't taste very nice. At the same time, it doesn't sound very reasonable to live on pure celery juice alone or experiment with unproven and unrealistic celery juice cleanses pushed by mainstream marketing, celebrities and hype gurus.

However, when done right, celery and celery juice can really help you take your health to the next level. This is why this book takes a different approach than most strict celery cleanse books out there.

It shows you how to incorporate celery into healthy and balanced, super low sugar and low carb juicing recipes to help you create optimal health. Without crazy cleanses. Without forcing yourself to drink juices that make you sick. Instead, you can enjoy all the benefits of celery in delicious, tasty and beautiful juices.

Green Juice Recipes That Don't Taste Gross - Introduction

Celery Juice Recipes That Don't Taste Gross are:

-low sugar and low carb (compatible with weight loss and low sugar diets)

-combine the healthiest low sugar fruits, veggies, superfoods, and herbs to help you create BALANCE

-taste delicious

This book is perfect if you want to:

-enjoy more energy, naturally

-give your body the nutrients it needs to stimulate healing

-speed up massive weight loss, naturally

-improve your health with easy to follow recipes

-have healthy-looking, glowing skin, strong nails, and shiny hair

Whether your goal is to lose weight, enjoy more energy, or learn a few delicious celery juice recipes- you have come to the right place.

With this book, you will discover how to juice the right way – the balanced way, so that you can enjoy all the benefits of celery juice as well as other amazing superfoods.

Green Juice Recipes That Don't Taste Gross - Introduction

In this book, the Celery is not playing solo...There is a whole team of amazing superfoods to make celery juice taste amazing so that you can enjoy more variety. You will never get bored with your juices.

The recipes contained in this book, are designed to help you:
1. Eliminate sugar cravings.
2. Start losing weight naturally.
3. Enjoy more energy and vibrant health.
4. Help your body heal naturally by giving it a myriad of nutrients to help it get back in balance it deserves.

<u>This guide is NOT designed as a juice fast.</u>
We recommend you follow a balanced, clean food diet with enough calories to meet your nutritional needs (you can check out the first book in the series called **Alkaline Ketogenic Mix** to learn delicious clean food, alkaline keto recipes you will never get bored with).

Then, treat juicing, in this case celery juicing as an additional wellness tool.

Celery is a Simple Superfood…

Most people think that healthy superfoods are super expensive, hard to pronounce, hard to find and totally unheard of.

Well, it doesn't have to be that way. There are many simple, common-sense superfoods that are easy to find (in your local grocery store) and can help you take your health to the next level.

The Benefits of Celery

Celery is very rich in:

-vitamin K (essential vitamin that is needed by the body for blood clotting and other important processes)

-vitamin A (healthy immune system, anti-age, and good vision)

-vitamins B-2 and B-6 (better nutrient absorption)

-vitamin C (healthy immune system and sustainable all-day energy)

Plus, it is also rich in:

-folate

-potassium

-manganese

-pantothenic acid

-dietary fiber

Celery is also low in calories and sugar, making it a perfect choice for a quick and healthy snack (I love snacking on celery sticks with some hummus or guacamole).

It's also an excellent juicing ingredient. When juicing, you give your digestive system a rest, and the nutrients absorb much quicker (and easier), because there is no fiber.

Juicing celery doesn't have to be boring. It can be exciting and fun!

Without any further ado, let's dive right into the food lists...

Juicing Recipes- Food Lists

(aside from our main hero, Celery)

Recommended Fruit

For healthy juicing, we encourage you to stay away from sugar, including fruit that is high in sugar.

However, low-sugar fruits are allowed, and they will make your celery juice recipes taste great.

Low Sugar Fruit:
- Lime
- Lemon
- Grapefruit
- Tomato (yea, it's a fruit)
- Pomegranate

Other Fruit (in moderation)
- Orange
- Apple
- Peach

- Pineapple
- pear

Recommended Greens to Use in Your Juicing Recipes

- Spinach
- Kale
- Microgreens
- Swiss Chard
- Arugula
- Endive
- Romaine Lettuce
- (and of course, our main hero – Celery!)

+ other fresh leafy greens and greens as well as:

- Parsley
- Mint
- Cilantro

I prefer fresh greens to green powders…but…whenever I go traveling, or I am really pressed for time, I use a delicious green powder that contains 11 superfoods. 11 in 1!

Green Juice Recipes That Don't Taste Gross - Introduction

I also like to add it to my recipes as it makes my juices taste really nice while adding a ton of superfoods at the same time. You can learn more about it and how I use it with my recipes on my website (treat it as an additional recommendation):

www.yourwellnessbooks.com/resources

Vegetables to Use in Your Juices:

- Red bell pepper
- Green bell pepper
- Yellow bell pepper
- Zucchini
- Broccoli
- Asparagus
- Colliflower
- Garlic
- Cucumbers
- Radishes

Spices & Herbs for Your Juices

The following herbs and spices will make your juices taste delicious. They are also full of anti-inflammatory properties:

- Cinnamon
- Himalaya Salt
- Curry
- Red Chili Powder
- Cumin
- Nutmeg
- Italian spices
- Oregano
- Rosemary
- Lavender
- Mint
- Chamomile
- Fennel
- Cilantro
- Moringa

Natural Sweeteners and Supplements (Optional)

Stevia (very helpful if you want to make a sweet juice without using sugar or sugar-containing foods or supplements)

- Green Powders
- Spirulina
- Chlorella
- Matcha
- Moringa Powder
- Maca Powder
- Ashwagandha Powder

Again, these are all optional. However, if you are interested in learning more, please visit our private website where I share more complimentary info with my readers. I have listed my favorite brands, green powders, and other health supplements to help you save your time on research:

www.YourWellnessBooks.com/resources

Good Fats

These will help your body in better nutrient absorption:

- Olive oil (organic, cold-pressed)
- Avocado oil
- Hemp oil
- Flaxseed oil
- Coconut oil
- Sesame oil

(please note, there is no need to purchase all of them, one, or two is enough; my two favorites are coconut oil and olive oil)

Other:

While these are not the main ingredients, they do work really well for some recipes. For example, some juicing recipes may taste way too intense, and so it makes sense to mix them with some healthy nut milk. For example, coconut or cashew milk can make your celery juice recipes taste naturally sweet and creamy.

- Almond milk
- Coconut milk
- Hazelnut milk
- Coconut water
- Herbal infusions
- Organic Apple Cider Vinegar

+ coffee and caffeine, in moderation (for example, you can combine your juice with a little bit of green tea or red tea to get you going in the morning!)

If you have any questions about the food lists for alkaline keto juices, please email me:
info@yourwellnessbooks.com

Your Wellness Books Email Newsletter

Before we dive into the recipes, we would like to offer you FREE access to our VIP Wellness Newsletter.

www.yourwellnessbooks.com/newsletter

Here's what's in for you:

-healthy, clean food recipes and tips delivered to your email

-motivation and inspiration to help you stay on track

-discounts and giveaways

-notifications about our new books (at massively reduced prices)

-healthy eating resources to help you on your journey

No Fluff, no spam. Only helpful and easy to follow info!

www.yourwellnessbooks.com/email-newsletter

Sign up link (copy this link to your phone, tablet, or PC):

Problems with signing up? Email us at info@yourwellnessbooks.com

About the Recipes-Measurements Used in the Recipes

The cup measurement I use is the American Cup measurement.

I also use it for dry ingredients. If you are new to it, let me help you:

If you don't have American Cup measures, just use a metric or imperial liquid measuring jug and fill your jug with your ingredient to the corresponding level. Here's how to go about it:

1 American Cup= 250ml= 8 Fl.oz.

For example:
If a recipe calls for 1 cup of almonds, simply place your almonds into your measuring jug until it reaches the 250 ml/8oz marks.

I hope you found it helpful. I know that different countries use different measurements, and I wanted to make things simple for you. I have also noticed that very often those who are used to American Cup measurements complain about metric measurements and vice versa. However, if you apply what I have just explained, you will find it easy to use both.

Celery Juice Recipes to Help You Thrive!

The golden rule is- when juicing, focus on:

-all kinds of veggies and greens that can be juiced

-low sugar fruit (for example lemons, limes, pomegranates, grapefruits)

Tips for getting started with juicing:

- Prepare your house: Clean out the fridge and pantry and be sure it's stocked with tons of fresh and frozen produce.
- Begin by adding a handful or so of organic baby spinach into your juices, especially if you're new to green juices.
- Invest in a good juicer and set an intention (for example: "I can't wait to get started on this journey and to juice 3 times a week" – is a simple to follow through goal and intention).
- Prepare all your juices the night before and store them in air-tight containers for the following day. Making all the juices at once can save time in clean up and ensures you're ready with fresh juice whenever needed.
- There are so many variations of juicing, you can use the recipes and add or take away ingredients. Feel free to swap for your favorite ingredients, just make sure you're getting a tasty variety throughout the day.

Celery Juice Recipes That Don't Taste Gross

The juicer I like to use is Omega Juicer. However, any other cold pressed juicer will do.

You can learn more about the recommended tools and resources at:

www.YourWellnessBooks.com/resources

Make sure you wash all the ingredients before you proceed to your juicing rituals.

Now, it's time for the recipes. I am so excited for you!

Recipe#1 Avocado Oil Celery Juice for Energy & Weight Loss

Avocado oil offers good fat to help you absorb the minerals and vitamins from the juice. I love this juice whenever I need "an injection of energy." Himalaya salt adds alkaline minerals and makes this juice taste amazing. If you like spicy juices, feel free to add in some hot sauce, or chili powder.

Servings: 2

Ingredients:

- 1 lemon, peeled
- 1 lime, peeled
- 6 celery stalks, chopped
- a handful of arugula leaves
- 2 big cucumbers, peeled and chopped
- 2 tablespoons avocado oil
- Himalayan salt to taste
- Optional: hot habanero sauce or chili powder

Instructions:

1. Place through a juicer.
2. Juice and combine with the avocado oil and Himalayan salt.
3. Serve in a glass and enjoy!

Celery Juice Recipes That Don't Taste Gross

Recipe#2 Quit Sugar Cravings Juice

This celery juice recipe is beginner friendly, and it's also designed to help you fight sugar cravings.

The creamy consistency of this juice, micronutrients from green juice and super healthy fats from coconut oil will help you say no to sugar.

Serves: 2

Ingredients:

- Half cup celery leaves
- 2-inch ginger, peeled
- 2 tablespoons melted coconut oil
- 1 cup of thick coconut milk
- Half teaspoon Ashwagandha
- Optional: stevia to sweeten

Instructions:

1. Place the celery and ginger through a juicer.
2. Extract the juice, pour it in a big glass.
3. Combine with coconut milk and oil.
4. Add in the Ashwagandha.
5. Stir well and enjoy.

Celery Juice Recipes That Don't Taste Gross

Recipe#3 Celery Juice Glow

This recipe uses turmeric that is very alkalizing and also offers anti-inflammatory benefits.

When peeling, cutting and juicing turmeric, I recommend you use gloves (unless you want to walk around with orange nails and hands for the next 2 days lol).

Servings: 2

Ingredients:

- 2 big red bell peppers, chopped
- Half cup celery leaves
- 2 inches of turmeric, peeled (use gloves)
- Half lemon
- 2 tablespoons flax seed oil

Instructions:

1. Juice all the ingredients using a juicer.
2. Add in the flax seed oil.
3. Serve in a glass.
4. Enjoy!

Recipe#4 Celery Immune Tonic

This recipe helps maintain a healthy immune system while helping you enjoy more energy (thanks to Vitamin C).

Servings: 2

Ingredients:

- half cup celery leaves
- 1 orange, peeled and chopped
- 1 inch of ginger, peeled
- 1 cup of water
- Optional: stevia to sweeten

Instructions:

1. Place all the ingredients in a juicer. Juice.
2. Mix with water.
3. Serve chilled with some ice cubes.
4. Enjoy!

Recipe#5 Super Hydrating Weight Loss Juice

This simple recipe is another easy to follow option for those who don't enjoy drinking pure celery juice. Cucumbers taste really delicious in juices and combine really well with coconut oil and milk.

Servings: 2

Ingredients:

- 4 big cucumbers, peeled and chopped
- 4 big carrots
- 5 celery sticks
- 2 tablespoons coconut oil, melted
- Himalaya salt to taste, if needed
- Half cup thick coconut milk

Instructions:

1. Place all the ingredients through a juicer.
2. Extract the juice.
3. Pour into a chilled glass.
4. Add in the coconut oil and coconut milk.
5. Taste with Himalaya salt if needed.
6. Enjoy!

Recipe#6 Holistic Balance Celery Juice

Celery offers anti-inflammatory properties and Vitamin C to help you enjoy more energy and take care of your immune system. Maca powder is a fantastic hormone balancer, and I love using it with this juice. Red bell pepper makes it taste really delicious, and so does the cinnamon and nutmeg powder.

Servings: 2

Ingredients:

- 1 cup celery, chopped
- 1 inch of ginger, peeled
- 1 red bell pepper
- 2 tablespoons avocado oil
- half teaspoon cinnamon powder
- half teaspoon maca powder
- cinnamon and nutmeg powder to taste

Instructions:

1. Juice all the ingredients using a juicer.
2. Pour in a glass.
3. Add in the avocado oil, maca, cinnamon, and nutmeg powder.
4. Stir well, serve and enjoy!

Recipe#7 On the Go Celery Juice Shot (Liver Lover)

This simple recipe helps detoxify the liver and it works really well first thing in the morning.

Serves: 1

Ingredients:

- 1 grapefruit
- Half cup celery leaves
- 1 tablespoon avocado oil or coconut oil
- Half cup coconut milk
- Stevia to sweeten, if needed

Instructions:

1. Juice grapefruit and celery.
2. In a small glass, combine the juice with the rest of the ingredients.
3. Stir well, drink, and enjoy!
4. To your health!

Recipe#8 Easy Energy Reboot Juice

This recipe uses coconut water to help you spice up your celery juice and make it taste amazing.

Serves: 1-2

Ingredients:

- 1 cup of coconut water
- 1 cup celery leaves
- 1-inch ginger
- 1 grapefruit, peeled
- Ice cubes

Instructions:

1. Juice the celery, ginger, and grapefruit.
2. Combine with coconut water and ice cubes.
3. Serve and enjoy!

Recipe#9 Aroma Detox Mix

Cabbage is an excellent source of sulfur, which helps purify the blood and detoxify the liver. Fennel and mint help create a nice flavor while adding in more healing nutrients to help you thrive.

Servings: 2

Ingredients:

- 1 small red cabbage
- 1 fennel bulb
- A handful of mint leaves
- A handful of celery leaves
- Half cup almond milk (or cashew milk)
- 2 tablespoons melted coconut oil
- Optional- stevia to sweeten

Procedure:

1. Juice all the ingredients.
2. Add the almond milk and coconut oil.
3. Stir well.
4. Enjoy!

Recipe#10 Vitamin C Celery Juice for Natural Energy & Weight Loss

This simple juice recipe offers a fantastic combination of greens with healthy, low sugar fruits and healthy fats. It will help you feel energized while eliminating sugar cravings.

Servings: 1-2

Ingredients:

- 2 grapefruits, peeled
- Half cup celery leaves
- 1-inch ginger
- Half cup coconut milk
- 2 tablespoon flax seed oil or sesame oil
- Optional: stevia to sweeten

Instructions:

1. Juice all the ingredients.
2. Combine with flax seed oil (or sesame oil).
3. If needed, sweeten with stevia.
4. Serve and enjoy!

Recipe#11 Light Alkaline Keto Juice

This juice is particularly useful for healthy eyesight and beautiful skin as it is packed with Vitamins A and C.

It also helps fight inflammation and takes care of your liver.

Ingredients:

- 1 cup radish, cut into smaller pieces
- 5 celery stalks, chopped
- 1-inch ginger
- half lime, peeled
- 1 cup coconut milk
- 1 tablespoon sesame or flax seed oil
- Pinch of Himalayan salt

Instructions:

1. Juice the radish, ginger, lime, and fennel.
2. Pour into a glass.
3. Add in the Himalayan salt and oil.
4. Stir in the coconut milk.
5. Stir well, serve and enjoy!

Recipe#12 Apple Cider Antioxidant Juice for Optimal Energy

This recipe is full of miraculous nutrients to help you get rid of toxins. Its therapeutic properties are enhanced by Apple Cider Vinegar.

Servings: 1-2

Ingredients:

- 2 cucumbers, peeled and sliced
- Half cup of celery leaves
- Half cup of mint leaves
- 2 tablespoons of olive oil
- 1 tablespoon apple cider vinegar (organic)
- Himalayan salt to taste (optional)

Instructions:

1. Juice all the ingredients.
2. Add in the olive oil, apple cider vinegar, Himalayan salt, and black pepper.
3. Serve and enjoy!

***To learn more about Apple Cider Vinegar (for health, home, and beauty), I highly recommend you read my book:

Apple Cider Vinegar: The Miraculous Natural Remedy!: Holistic Solutions & Proven Healing Recipes for Health, Beauty, and Home

If your goal is weight loss and body detoxification, you can start adding about 1-2 tablespoons (a day) of quality, organic, apple cider vinegar to your alkaline-keto drinks.

Apple cider vinegar goes really well with therapeutic alkaline keto juices (and also smoothies). It's inexpensive and very effective.

Recipe#13 Herbal Weight Loss Juice

This recipe fuses the low sugar alkaline fruits with horsetail infusion. Horsetail infusion is an excellent natural remedy to get rid of water retention, lose weight, and burn fat. It's full of alkaline minerals and blends really well with this juice.

Ingredients:

- A handful of fresh mint leaves
- A handful of celery leaves
- 1 grapefruit, cut into smaller pieces
- A green apple, cut into smaller pieces
- 1 lime, peeled
- Half inch ginger, peeled
- 1 cucumber, peeled and cut into smaller pieces
- Half cup horsetail infusion cooled down
- Optional: stevia to sweeten

Instructions:

1. First, juice all the ingredients.
2. Pour into a glass.
3. Combine with horsetail infusion. Add stevia if needed.
4. Serve and enjoy!

Recipe#14 Sleep Well Celery Juice

This delicious herbal juice uses verbena- a herb used to stimulate relaxation and peace of mind.

Servings: 1-2

Ingredients:

- 1 cup verbena infusion, cooled down a bit (use 1 teabag per cup)
- 2 grapefruits, peeled and sliced
- 1 apple, peeled and sliced
- A handful of chopped celery
- A handful of fresh mint leaves
- Stevia to sweeten

Procedure:

1. Juice the grapefruits, celery, and mint leaves.
2. Mix the juice with the infusion.
3. Stir well and add stevia for naturally sweet taste.
4. Enjoy!

Verbena is a pretty safe herb, but there is not enough information to confirm whether it can be used during pregnancy or breastfeeding. The same applies to possible contraindications with other medications. I always recommend consulting with your doctor first.

Recipe#15 Pomegranate Celery Anti-Sugar Cravings Juice

This recipe will help you get rid of sugar cravings while feeding your body with a myriad of nutrients it needs to thrive. Pomegranate juice is full of alkaline minerals as well as Vitamin C.

It's a natural antioxidant and anti-inflammatory. It blends really well with ginger, turmeric, and celery.

Servings: 2

Ingredients:

- 1 cup pomegranate seeds
- 1-inch ginger root, peeled
- 1-inch turmeric root, peeled
- A handful of celery leaves
- 2 tablespoons of avocado oil
- Stevia to sweeten (optional)

Procedure:

1. Juice the pomegranate seeds, ginger, turmeric, and celery.
2. Pour into a glass.
3. Combine with avocado oil.
4. Stir well.
5. Serve and enjoy!

Recipe#16 Alkalizing Mojito Juice

It's time for a simple and super healthy, non-alcoholic version of mojito!

Servings: 2-3

Ingredients:

- 1 cucumber, peeled and sliced
- Half cup fresh mint leaves
- Half cup celery leaves
- 2 limes, peeled and sliced
- A few mint leaves to garnish
- A few lime slices to garnish
- 3 cups alkaline (or filtered) water
- Stevia to sweeten (optional)

Instructions:

1. Juice all the ingredients (except the mint and lime slices for garnishing)
2. Pour the fresh juice into a tall water jar or pitcher.
3. Add fresh water and ice cubes.
4. Now, add the mint leaves and lime slices.
5. Stir in well, chill in a fridge for a few hours, and serve.
6. Enjoy!

Recipe #17 Cucumber Kale and Carrot Juice

While it's hard to eat a mountain of greens and cucumbers, it's easy to drink their juice and get all the vital nutrients in. Avocado oil offers good fat to help you absorb the minerals and vitamins from the juice.

Servings: 2

Ingredients:

- 2 big carrots, peeled and chopped
- 1 lemon, peeled
- 5 celery stalks, chopped
- A couple dashes of habanero hot sauce
- a handful of kale, chopped
- 2 big cucumbers, peeled and chopped
- a drizzle of avocado oil

Instructions:

1. Place through a juicer.
2. Juice.
3. Pour into a glass and add in a couple dashes of habanero hot sauce and avocado oil, if needed.

Recipe #18 Flavored Celery Juice

While pure celery juice can be a bit hardcore, this recipe is a bit different.

Add in some fresh apples and ginger and you will fall in love with green celery juice.

Serves: 2

Ingredients:

- 1 cup of celery leaves
- 2 green apples, peeled and chopped
- 2-inch ginger, peeled
- 1 tablespoon melted coconut oil

Instructions:

1. Place all the ingredients through a juicer.
2. Extract the juice, pour it in a big glass.
3. Add in some melted coconut oil.
4. Stir well and enjoy.

Recipe #19 Watermelon Antioxidant Juice

Watermelon, ginger and celery is an excellent combination. It makes the juice taste nice and helps you get accustomed to juicing celery.

Servings: 2

Ingredients:

- 1 cup of watermelon, chopped
- 1 cup celery leaves
- 2 inches of ginger, peeled

Instructions:

1. Juice all the ingredients using a juicer.
2. Serve in a glass.
3. Enjoy!

Recipe #20 Simple Apple Lemon Juice

Apples help maintain a healthy digestive system. Oh, and they make green juices taste great!

Servings: 2

Ingredients:

- 1 cups of celery leaves
- 2 apples, peeled and chopped
- 1 lemon, peeled and halved
- 1 inch of ginger, peeled
- 1-inch turmeric, peeled

Instructions:

1. Place all the ingredients in a juicer.
2. Juice and serve in a glass.
3. Enjoy!

Recipe #21 Honeydew Melon Green Juice

While a pure green celery juice may be a bit too much for a beginner, adding in some honeydew melon really takes it to a whole new level.

Servings: 2

Ingredients:

- 4 medium cucumbers, peeled and chopped
- 1 cup of honeydew melon
- 1 cup celery leaves

Instructions:

1. Place all the ingredients through a juicer.
2. Extract the juice.
3. Pour into a chilled glass and enjoy!

Recipe #22 Easy Celery Juice

Red bell peppers are one of my favorite veggies to juice.

They are natural sweet and full of vitamins and minerals. They make any green juice taste amazing. Ginger adds to anti-inflammatory properties.

Servings: 2

Ingredients:

- 1 cup celery, chopped
- 3 red bell peppers, chopped
- 1 inch of ginger, peeled
- 2 slices of lime, to garnish
- Fresh ice cubes

Instructions:

1. Juice all the ingredients using a juicer.
2. Pour in a glass, add in some ice cubes.
3. Garnish with lime slices.
4. Serve and enjoy!

Celery Juice Recipes That Don't Taste Gross

Recipe #23 Coconut Celery Concoction

Compared to other juicing recipes, this one is relatively simple and quick to make as it leverages the coconut water. Just perfect as a quick, energy boosting juice

Servings: 2

Ingredients:

- 1 cup celery leaves
- 1 green apple, cut into smaller pieces
- 1 cup of coconut water
- 1 teaspoon cinnamon powder

Instructions:

1. Juice the celery and apple.
2. Pour into a glass and mix with 1 cup of coconut water.
3. Stir well, add in 1 teaspoon of cinnamon powder and stir again.

Celery Juice Recipes That Don't Taste Gross

Recipe #24 Broccoli and Orange Juice

This juice is great for boosting your energy and stimulating weight loss.

It combines the healing and immune system boosting benefits of Vitamin C from oranges with the detoxifying properties of chlorophyll from the celery.

Servings: 2

Ingredients:

- 1 cup celery leaves
- 2 oranges, peeled and cut into smaller pieces
- 1 lemon, peeled and cut into smaller pieces
- 1-½ cups of alkaline water

Instructions:

1. Place through a juicer.
2. Juice, and pour into a jar or a big glass and add in some water (you can skip this step if you like the intense taste of this juice)
3. Enjoy!

Recipe #25 Green Tea High Energy Juice

This uses green tea to help you boost your energy levels and burn fat. Ginger adds to anti-inflammatory properties.

Servings: 2

Ingredients:

- 2 oranges, peeled and cut into smaller pieces
- 1 green apple, cut to smaller pieces
- Half cup celery leaves
- 1-inch ginger, peeled
- 1 cup green tea, cooled down

Instructions:

1. Juice the oranges, ginger and spinach.
2. Pour into a glass or a jar and add in some green tea.
3. Enjoy!

Recipe #26 A Beta Carotene Powerhouse

This juice is a fantastic combination of oranges, turmeric and carrots to help you have beautiful and healthy-looking skin while enjoying more energy without having to rely on caffeine.

Servings: 2

Ingredients:

- 6 carrots, peeled and chopped
- 2 oranges, peeled and cut into smaller pieces
- Half cup celery leaves
- 1 lemon, peeled and cut into smaller pieces
- 1 zucchini, peeled and cut into smaller pieces
- 2-inch turmeric, peeled
- A few ice cubes (optional)
- A dash of cinnamon powder (optional)

Instructions:

1. Juice all the ingredients.
2. Pour into a glass and add in some ice cubes and a dash of cinnamon powder.
3. Enjoy!

Recipe #27 A Restorative Antioxidant Juice

This juice is full of antioxidants and beta-carotene to help you have beautiful skin.

Servings: 2

Ingredients:

- 4 large carrots, peeled and chopped
- 4 tomatoes, cut into smaller pieces
- 6 celery sticks, chopped
- 1 garlic clove, peeled
- 1-inch ginger, peeled

Instructions:

1. Juice all the ingredients.
2. Pour into a glass and enjoy!

Celery Juice Recipes That Don't Taste Gross

Recipe #28 Veggie Medley Juice

Enjoy the wonderful mixture full of ingredients that make you healthy. They also contain antioxidant and elements that will help your body to fight against diseases and help in weight loss.

Servings: 4

Ingredients:

- 6 medium carrots, peeled and cut into smaller pieces
- 1 beet peeled and cut into smaller pieces
- 3 large tomatoes, cut into smaller pieces
- 1 red bell pepper, chopped
- 4 large celery stalks, chopped

Instructions:

1. Juice all the ingredients.
2. Pour into a glass.
3. If needed, season with some Himalaya salt.
4. Enjoy!

Recipe #29 Coconut Flavored Antioxidant Juice

This recipe has plenty of antioxidants and is full of refreshing nutrients.

While pure green celery juice might be a bit too "hardcore" even for experienced juicing fanatics, it tastes amazing when mixed with other ingredients.

Servings: 1

Ingredients:

- Half cup celery leaves
- Half cup coconut water or coconut milk
- 2 green apples, chopped

Instructions:

1. Juice all the ingredients.
2. Pour into a glass and mix with some coconut water.
3. Enjoy!

Recipe #30 Mixed Green Juice

This recipe is great if you happen to have some arugula leaves leftovers and don't feel like going for another salad. And yes, arugula juice tastes amazing when mixed with other ingredients!

Servings: 2

Ingredients:

- 1 cup arugula leaves
- A few pineapples slices
- 4 celery sticks, chopped
- 1 orange, peeled and cut into smaller pieces
- 1 green apple, peeled and cut into smaller pieces

Instructions:

1. Place though a juicer.
2. Juice and pour into a glass or a small jar.
3. Enjoy!

Recipe #31 Tantalizing Green Juice

Once again, we are juicing arugula leaves while adding in some sweetness and vitamin C from Kiwis and anti-inflammatory benefits of ginger. Apple helps in digestion and lime adds even more of vitamin C and refreshing aroma.

Servings: 2

Ingredients:

- 1 cup arugula leaves
- Half cup celery leaves
- 2 kiwis, peeled
- 1 green apple, cut into smaller pieces
- 1 lime, peeled and cut into smaller pieces
- 1-inch ginger, peeled

Instructions:

1. Place all the ingredients though a juicer.
2. Juice and enjoy!

Recipe #32 Healing Carrot Juice

Carrot juice tastes amazing and when combined with cucumber juice, it will help you stay hydrated and reduce unwanted sugar cravings for hours. Ashwagandha powder is optional here. But it's a great choice to help you re-balance your energy levels while feeling more relaxed.

Servings: 2

Ingredients:

- 6 carrots, peeled and chopped
- 3 big cucumbers, peeled and chopped
- Half cup celery leaves
- ¼ teaspoon Ashwagandha powder

Instructions:

1. Juice all the ingredients.
2. Pour into a glass and enjoy!

Recipe #33 Cucumber's Delight

Cucumber contains water that provides a good environment for hydration and therefore contributes to weight loss. Parsley leaves add in a ton of vitamins and nutrients such as Vitamin A, Vitamin C and Iron. Mint helps in digestion and brings an amazing aroma to the table.

Servings: 2

Ingredients:

- 2 large cucumbers, peeled and chopped
- A handful of fresh mint leaves
- A handful of fresh parsley leaves
- A handful of fresh celery leaves
- Half cup coconut or cashew milk

Instructions:
1. Juice all the ingredients.
2. Pour into a glass or a small jar and mix with coconut or cashew milk.
3. Enjoy!

Recipe #34 Turmeric Celery Juice

Turmeric is full of polyphenols that help well in weight loss. It's a great addition to your juices and creates a nice, spicy aroma that is very easy to get hooked on.

Servings: 2

Ingredients:

- 2-inch turmeric, peeled
- 2-inch ginger, peeled
- 4 celery stalks, chopped
- 2 oranges, peeled and cut into smaller pieces
- 1 lemon, peeled and cut into smaller pieces
- Half cup water, filtered

Instructions:

1. Juice all the ingredients.
2. Pour into a glass and mix with water.
3. Enjoy!

Recipe #35 Pineapple Lime Mint Juice

This recipe balances the energy and weight loss stimulating benefits of greens with the sweetness of pineapple.

Servings: 3-4

Ingredients:

- half cup celery, chopped
- half cup pineapple, chopped
- half cup mint leaves, fresh
- 2 limes, peeled and chopped

Instructions:

1. Place through a juicer.
2. Juice and pour into a glass.
3. Enjoy!

Recipe #36 Antioxidant Nutrition Juice

With orange pomegranate, you are sure of enjoying juice that is full of antioxidants and nutrients that are good for weight loss.

Servings: 2

Ingredients:

- 1 cup pomegranate seeds
- 1 cup of celery leaves
- 2 oranges, peeled and cut into smaller pieces

Instructions:

1. Place through a juicer.
2. Pour into a glass and enjoy!

Recipe #37 Coconut Flavored Green Juice

The ingredients are rich in phytonutrients and antioxidants. The juice relaxes the body and makes it easy to lose extra pounds.

Servings: 2

Ingredients:

- 1 cup celery leaves
- 2 tablespoons avocado oil
- 1 cup pineapple, chopped
- 1 green apple, chopped

Instructions:

1. Place all the ingredients through a juicer.
2. Juice and pour into a glass
3. Enjoy!

Recipe#38 Creamy, Anti-Inflammatory Breakfast Delight

Yes, this juice is great as a natural drink. It is packed with nutrients, and uses an army of anti-inflammatory spices.

Servings: 1-2

Ingredients:

- 2 beets, peeled
- 1 red apple, peeled
- 2 red bell peppers
- 1 cup celery leaves
- 1-inch ginger, peeled
- 1 cup coconut milk or coconut cream (natural, organic)
- 2 tablespoons of coconut oil
- 2 tablespoons of chia seeds
- Stevia to sweeten (optional)
- Half teaspoon cinnamon powder
- Half teaspoon nutmeg powder

Instructions:

1. Wash and chop the veggies.
2. Juice and add some ginger too.
3. Mix the fresh juice with coconut milk (or coconut cream, just be sure to choose coconut milk that has a thick consistency).

4. Add the cinnamon and nutmeg powder. Sweeten with stevia. Stir well.
5. Place 2 tablespoons of chia seeds on top.

Recipe#39 Get Energized Antioxidant Juice

I don't know about you, but I love combining my juices with teas and herbal infusions. Especially green tea!

Perfect recipe to help you stay energized for hours, without getting overstimulated.

Servings: 1-2

Ingredients:

- 1 cup of green tea, cooled down
- 2 oranges
- A handful of celery leaves
- Optional: stevia to sweeten if needed

Instructions:

1. Juice the celery and oranges.
2. Combine with green tea, serve and enjoy!

Recipe#40 Green Balance Party Juice

Fennel bulb is naturally sweet and can be an amazing addition to your celery juices. It is also rich in potassium, vitamin A, calcium, iron, vitamin B6, magnesium, as well as phosphorus, zinc, copper, selenium, beta-carotene and manganese.

Servings: 2

Ingredients:

- 4 big cucumbers, peeled
- Half cup celery leaves
- Half fennel bulb
- 1 -inch ginger, peeled
- 1 big, ripe pear to taste
- Half cup water, filtered, preferably alkaline

Instructions:

1. Wash and chop all the veggies.
2. Peel the cucumber, lemon and ginger.
3. Place through a juicer.
4. Add some water.
5. Stir well, drink and enjoy!

Recipe#41 Delicious Creamy Beet Juice

Beets are rich in antioxidant and anti-inflammatory phytonutrients, like betalains. Moreover, beetroot is also a diuretic, helping fight water retention, edema, and cellulite.

Servings: 2-3

Ingredients:

- half cup celery leaves
- 2 beets (with the leaves if possible)
- 1 apple, peeled
- 2 carrots, peeled, unless organic
- 2 limes, peeled
- half teaspoon powdered cinnamon
- half cup coconut milk

Instructions:

1. Juice all the ingredients.
2. Now, stir in the cinnamon powder.
3. Mix with coconut milk, serve and enjoy!

Recipe#42 Spicy Green Celery Juice

This juice can be a fantastic, natural remedy for colds and flu.

Servings: 1-2

Ingredients:

- Half inch turmeric root, peeled
- Half inch ginger root, peeled
- 1 red bell pepper
- half cup celery leaves
- 1 big tomato
- 1 lime, peeled

Instructions:

1. Wash and chop all the ingredients.
2. Juice and enjoy!

Recipe #43 Gazpacho Celery Juice

This recipe tastes a bit like Spanish gazpacho and can get you hooked on celery…

Serves: 1

Ingredients:

- 2 big tomatoes
- 2 big cucumbers, peeled
- 4 celery sticks, chopped
- 1 tablespoon olive oil
- Himalayan salt and black pepper to taste

Instructions:

1. Juice all the ingredients.
2. Add in olive oil, Himalayan salt and black pepper.
3. Stir well, serve and enjoy!

Recipe #44 "Replenish Yourself" Juice

Coconut water can be a great addition to your celery juicing recipes. It's excellent for optimal hydration and it contains many natural minerals, such as Magnesium.

Serves: 2-3

Ingredients:

- 1 cup coconut water
- 2-inch ginger
- 1 garlic clove, peeled
- 2 grapefruits
- 1 cup celery leaves

Instructions:

1. Juice all the ingredients.
2. Combine with coconut water and ice cubes.
3. Serve and enjoy!

Recipe #45 "Red Pepper Detox" Juice

Fennel and mint help create a sweet flavor while contributing more healing nutrients to help you thrive.

Servings: 2

Ingredients:

- 2 big red bell peppers
- 1 fennel bulb
- A handful of mint leaves (optional)
- 1 cup celery leaves
- Half cup of coconut milk
- 1 tablespoon avocado oil
- Optional- stevia to sweeten

Instructions:

1. Juice all the ingredients.
2. Add the coconut milk and avocado oil.
3. Stir well, adding stevia if needed.
4. Enjoy!

Recipe #46 "Liver Lover" Juice

Grapefruits are very rich in phytonutrients called limonoids that promote the production of antioxidant enzymes. These help the liver to remove toxic compounds easier, thereby protecting the liver in the process.

Servings: 2

Ingredients:

- 2 grapefruits, peeled
- Half cup celery leaves
- 1 inch of fresh root ginger, peeled
- Half cup water, filtered, preferably alkaline
- 2 tablespoons of Udo's Choice (you can also use cold-pressed flax oil)
- Pinch of Himalayan salt
- 1 tablespoon of avocado or olive oil

Instructions:

1. Juice all the ingredients.
2. Add the water, Udo's Choice, Himalayan salt and olive or avocado oil.
3. Stir well and drink to your health.

Celery Juice Recipes That Don't Taste Gross

Recipe #47 Creamy Chia Juice

What I really like about this recipe is its natural creaminess thanks to cashew milk and chia seeds.

Servings: 2-3

Ingredients:

- 2 cucumbers, peeled
- 1-inch ginger, peeled
- Half cup celery leaves
- 1 tablespoon avocado oil or olive oil
- 1 cup of raw cashew milk (unsweetened)
- Pinch of black pepper and Himalayan salt if needed

Instructions:

1. Juice the cucumbers, ginger and celery.
2. Pour into a glass.
3. Stir in some olive or avocado oil and mix in the cashew milk while adding black pepper and Himalayan salt.
4. Drink immediately.
5. Enjoy the energy!

Let's finish this book with a few words of motivation and inspiration.

It's all about taking meaningful and inspired action.

Ditch perfection for progress. Focus on daily micro steps. Healthy choices. Ask yourself- is this taking me closer to my goals?

Cultivate positive self-talk. Stop beating yourself up.

Beautiful results will start taking place.

Think where you will be 5 years from now…The baby steps will compound into a big transformation.

Be patient. Focus on the here and now.

Thank you again for reading.

I am really grateful for you,

Until next time,

Wishing you all the best on your journey,

Elena

www.amazon.com/author/elenagarcia

Final Words

We Need Your Help

One more thing, before you go, could you please do us a quick favor?

It would be great if you could leave us a short review online.

Don't worry, it doesn't have to be long. One sentence is enough.

Let others know your favorite recipes and who you think this book can help.

Way too many people drink "normal" juices and don't even realize they are overdoing sugar…No wonder they give up…

Your review can inspire more and more people to learn the right method of juicing, that they can finally achieve their wellness and weight loss goals the way they deserve.

Thank You for your support!

Final Words

Join Our VIP Readers' Newsletter to Boost Your Wellbeing

Would you like to be notified about our new health and wellness books?

How about receiving them at deeply discounted prices? And before anyone else?

What about awesome giveaways, latest health tips, and motivation?

If that is something you are interested in, please visit the link below to join our newsletter:

www.yourwellnessbooks.com/email-newsletter

It's 100% free + spam free (we hate spam as much as you do)

We promise we will only email you with valuable and relevant information, delicious recipes, and tips to help you on your journey.

Sign up link:

www.yourwellnessbooks.com/email-newsletter

Final Words

More Wellness Books & Resources

Available at:

www.yourwellnessbooks.com

Content Disclaimer

The information contained in this book is for informational and educational purposes only.

It is not an attempt by the writers or publisher to diagnose or prescribe, nor should it be construed to be such.

Readers are hereby encouraged to consult with a licensed health care professional concerning the information presented, which has been received from sources deemed reliable, but no guarantees, expressed or implied, can be made regarding the accuracy of same.

Therefore, readers are also encouraged to verify for themselves and to their own satisfaction the accuracy of all reports, recommendations, conclusions, comments, opinions, or anything else published herein before making any kind of decisions based upon what they have read.

If you have a medical condition, please consult your medical practitioner.